Do Animals Think?

Sarah Fleming

Contents

Have you ever licked a cut?

Introduction

Animals lick their cuts, too. It's a good idea. Licking a cut covers it in **saliva**. Saliva has things in it that can help cuts heal, and kill **microbes**.

Definition

Saliva (say sal-i-vah) saliva is liquid in a person's or animal's mouth

Microbe (say mike-robe) a living thing that is so small you need a microscope to see it. Some microbes can infect cuts.

Sick animals often find somewhere safe to hide and rest while they get better.

Just like we do!

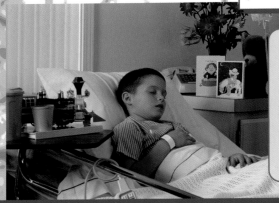

Do animals know that licking and resting is good for them, or do they just do it? *Do animals think?*

Do Animals Think?

Do you think animals think?

No it's just **instinct**.

 People have been asking this question for a long time.

Definition

instinct: something people and animals know how to do without learning it

 Some people say animals do everything by instinct.

Does a spider *think* about spinning a web, or does it just do it by instinct?

Others say that animals can think.

This crow figured out that to get to the food in the tube, it needed to bend the wire first to make a hook.

Health Good Food

Animals need to eat well to stay healthy. They need extra food sometimes, such as when they are feeding their young. So animals go and look for foods that have the things they need in them.

People and animals need **minerals** in their **diet**. Minerals come from the ground and can be found in many foods. Calcium is a mineral. It is found in milk. Bones are made of calcium. Young animals need calcium to help their bones grow.

Definition

diet: the food you normally eat

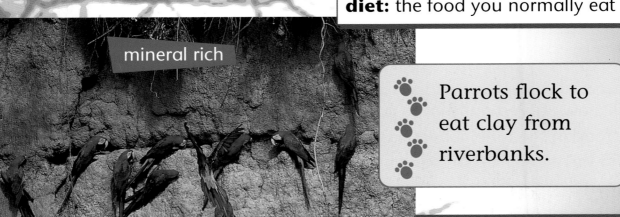

mineral rich

Parrots flock to eat clay from riverbanks.

Many animals need salt in their diet. These goats are licking salt off a road. People put the salt on the road to keep it from getting icy.

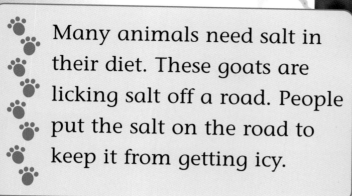

mineral rich

Some deer will eat old antlers as their new ones are growing. This gives them all the minerals they need to make the new ones.

Elephants walk hundreds of miles to these caves. They dig into the walls of the caves and eat the rocky soil.

mineral rich

Do they know it's good for them?

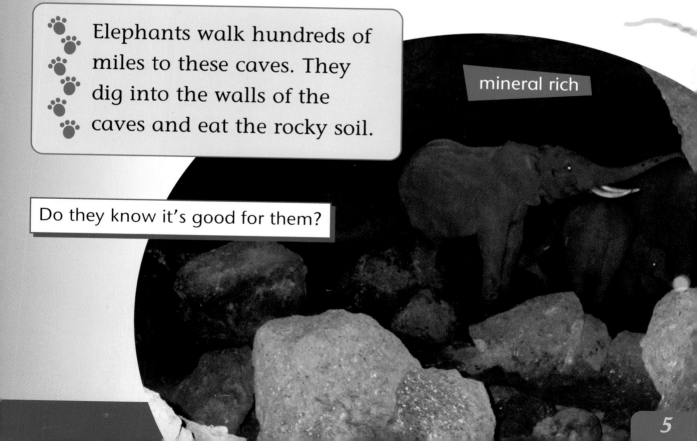

Keeping Clean

 Animals groom themselves to keep clean. Being clean helps animals stay healthy.

 Some animals **groom** themselves.

Definition

groom: to make someone or something clean

 Some animals are groomed by their friends.

Some animals are groomed by other kinds of animals.

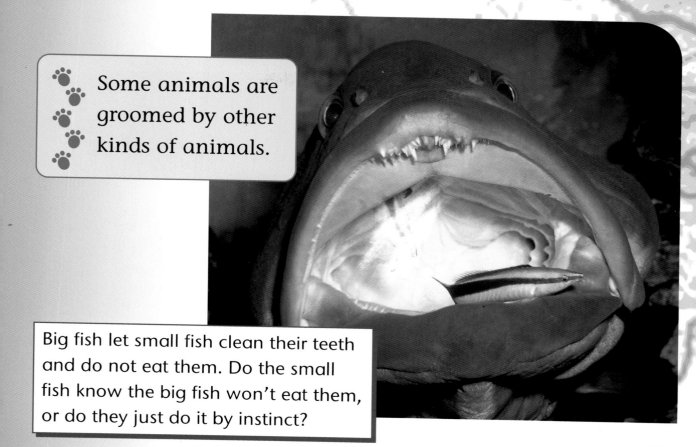

Big fish let small fish clean their teeth and do not eat them. Do the small fish know the big fish won't eat them, or do they just do it by instinct?

Animals also groom themselves to get rid of bugs that might have gotten on their skin.

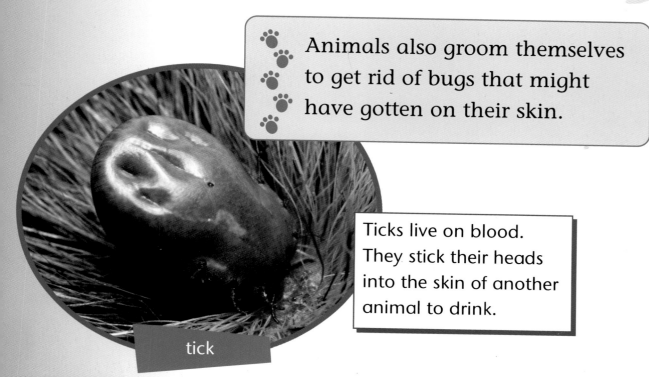

tick

Ticks live on blood. They stick their heads into the skin of another animal to drink.

Biting Insects

 People and animals try not to get sick. Sometimes, however, people and animals get bitten by insects that can make them ill.

horsefly

mosquito

flea

There are more than 2,000 different types of flea that eat birds and mammals.

This water buffalo is rolling in mud to keep insects away (it's cool, too).

Some animals have long tails or thick skins like rhinoceroses. These help protect them from biting insects. Still, even very thick-skinned animals roll in mud.

Tigers can spend most of the day in water. It keeps insects away (and it's cool).

These bears rub their skin on sticky pine trees. The sticky sap keeps flies away.

 Hedgehogs rub mint leaves or fruit into their spines to kill **lice**.

Definition

lice: small animals with eight legs that live on the blood of other animals. The singular for *lice* is *louse*.

 People put repellent on their skin to keep insects from biting them.

Where in the World?

Animals are very good at knowing where they are. They can travel a long way to get home.

homing pigeon

The record distance for a homing pigeon to get home is 1,004 miles (1,610 km).

Some swallows go back to the same nest after flying more than 1,000 miles (1,600 km).

Key

Migration routes of some European swallows

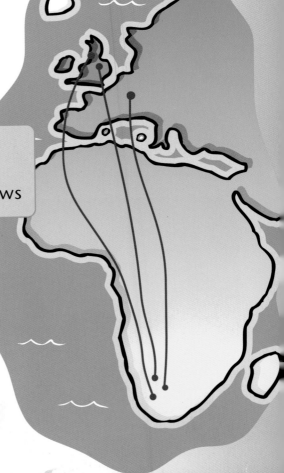

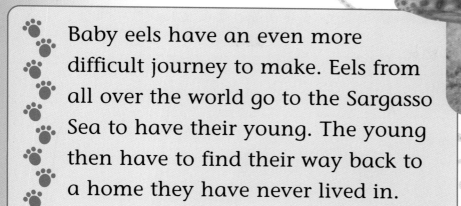

Baby eels have an even more difficult journey to make. Eels from all over the world go to the Sargasso Sea to have their young. The young then have to find their way back to a home they have never lived in.

When animals travel a long distance every year, it is called migration.

Sargasso Sea

Key

Home rivers and coasts of eels all around the North Atlantic Ocean.

Sargasso Sea, where all these eels migrate to lay their eggs.

Place and Memory

 Some animals have very good memories.

Do you think they can remember the elephant who died?

 Elephants remember where other members of their herd have died. They go back to that place and feel the bones.

 Old elephants are useful to the herd because they can remember where the best watering holes are when there is no rain.

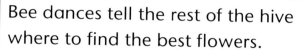

Bee dances tell the rest of the hive where to find the best flowers.

Squirrels remember where they hid their food.

This bird stores about 30,000 seeds in autumn, and can remember where about 20,000 of them are the next spring.

Tools

People used to say that only humans used **tools**. However, many animals also use tools.

We people use tools. It shows we're better than the animals.

Some birds use stones to break open snail shells and other birds' eggs.

Some animals use sticks or spines to get little animals out of holes.

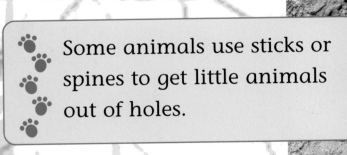

Some animals even make umbrellas!

Sea otters crack open shellfish with a stone. Sea otters have favorite stones, and they tuck the stone under their arms when they dive for food.

Learning

 Animals can learn how to do things by watching other animals, or by being taught by people.

Cheetah cubs are taught to hunt by their mother. If she dies before they learn, they will starve.

This robin learned how to fish by watching a kingfisher.

This dog has learned to sniff out people trapped by an **earthquake**.

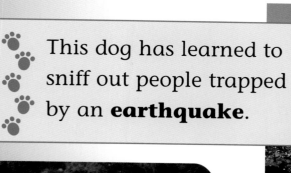

This bear has learned how to "dance" to get money for its owner. Sadly, bears are beaten and starved when they don't do what the trainer wants.

Talking

These monkeys call out when other animals attack them. The call for "eagle" is different from the call for "snake." When they hear the "eagle" call, monkeys hide in bushes, but "SNAKE!!" makes them climb tall trees.

A fur seal mother comes back from fishing and has to find her cub among a huge crowd of up to a million seals. She can do this because she recognizes its call from among all the other calling seals. People can do this, too. Have you ever heard your name spoken across a crowded room? Your brain is tuned to hearing it, even in a babble of noise.

Elephants can hear each other calling from two and a half miles (4 km) away.

Whales sing to each other from hundreds of miles away.

Kanzi, an ape, has been taught to "talk" in picture language. She can "speak" 200 words, and understands about 500 words.

This parrot learned 1,000 English words.

Prediction

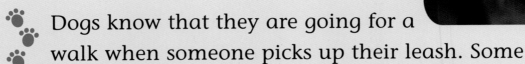

Dogs know that they are going for a walk when someone picks up their leash. Some animals can **predict** what is going to happen.

Is this just because animals have better hearing and other senses than people?

The Legend of the Freiburg Duck

During World War II, the German city of Freiburg was going to be bombed. When the bombers were still far away, before any warning sirens went off, a duck started flapping and quacking in such a way that the people living near it got frightened and went to hide in shelters. That night, November 11, 1944, most of Freiburg was bombed, and people say that they lived through it thanks to the duck.

Once, in Roman times, soldiers were woken by geese honking. The soldiers found that they were under attack!

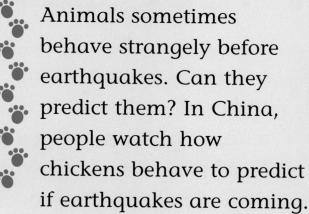

Animals sometimes behave strangely before earthquakes. Can they predict them? In China, people watch how chickens behave to predict if earthquakes are coming.

Animals "Predicted Quake"

■ Jagdish Singh, Kankaria, India

YESTERDAY'S EARTHQUAKE caught everyone by surprise. Everyone, that is, except the animals at the local zoo. Minutes before the quake, zookeepers reported that their wild animals had really "gone wild." Frantic birds beat against their cages, otters dashed out of their ponds, snakes slid out of their holes, big cats prowled.

Strangest of all were the elephants – some spread their legs wide to balance, others lay down and held onto things with their trunks. The zoo suffered badly in the earthquake.

A Test Case

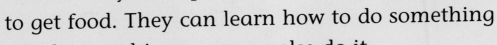

 Octopuses are very smart. They can go through mazes. They can open jars to get food. They can learn how to do something new by watching someone else do it.

This octopus is pulling out the stopper to get to its lunch.

Look Back

1 Give an example of an animal predicting something.

2 How do cheetah cubs know how to hunt?

3 Which tool do sea otters use? What do they use it for?

4 Why do animals roll in mud?

Index

Glossary

diet — what you normally eat

earthquake — a violent movement of part of the Earth's surface

instinct — a natural thing to do or feel

microbe — a living thing that is so small you need a microscope to see it

migration — to go and live in another part of the same country, or a different country, usually for part of the year

mineral — a hard material that can be dug out of the ground, such as coal

predict — to say or guess that something will happen in the future

tool — an object used to help you do something